Wolves in Yellowstone

The Humane Society of the United States

Written and Illustrated
by: Randy Houk

*for Tom Hudson, with love
and gratitude for endless
encouragement*

Back in eighteen eighty-two
There were wolves in Yellowstone;
Black and gray and silver-blue,
Wolves in packs and wolves alone.

2

When the silver moon was round,
Packs would gather, packs would howl.
Such a sad, sweet, longing sound;
Not coyote, not like owl.

3

Herds of elk lived in the park;
Bison, pronghorn, moose and deer.
You could hear coyotes bark,
When a night was cold and clear.

Grizzlies roamed in Yellowstone,
They too hunted elk and deer.
It was not the wolf alone
Many people came to fear.

Wolves are rarely even seen.
Wolves avoid men, try to run.

Wolves don't kill just to be mean –
Wolves must hunt for food, not fun.

5

Wolves have golden-yellow eyes,
Haunting eyes that almost glow.
Wolves are shy and wolves are wise:
Why did people fear them so?

Came the ranches – came the farm.
Wolves are predators, and so,
Thinking stock would come to harm,
Someone said, "Those wolves must go."

And by nineteen thirty-five,
Once the hunting was all done,
No more wolves were left alive.
Wolves were gone: Each pack, each one.

Years went by in Yellowstone.
Sometimes, someone saw a track,
Just a footprint – all alone.
Might the wolves be coming back?

But not one gray wolf remained.
And by nineteen thirty-eight
Nearly every wolf was slain,
Gone in almost every state.

□Endangered List
bald eagle
elephant
gray wolf
kangaroo rat
Mountain gorilla
giant Panda
galapagos tortoise
white rhinocerous
Indian elephant
____der crocodile
____ whale
____oping crane
tapir
grizzly bear
manatee
florida panther

Wolves were added to the list:
The endangered list just grew.
Many animals were missed;
Many species, not a few.

Those who worked at Yellowstone
Wrote and talked and worked for years,
Hoping people could be shown
How unreal were most wolf fears.

And The Wolf Fund gave the facts,
Helping people lose their fright.
They helped people want wolves back:
Want to set the balance right.

11

And in nineteen ninety-five
You could hear the trailer drone,
Bringing fourteen wolves, alive -
Bringing wolves to Yellowstone.

Wolves were brought in metal crates.
Wolves were brought from way up North.
Children lined the entrance gates,
Clapping, as the truck came forth.

Each wolf wore a radio collar,
So when freed in Yellowstone,
Rangers would know how to follow,
And would know how far they'd roam.

They weren't freed at first, for fear
Those wolves would go north again.
Fed on car-killed elk and deer,
Each pack stayed inside a pen.

Late that still and starry night,
Thirteen crates were opened up.
Most wolves froze inside with fright:
One wolf bolted with her pup.

Velvet black was her coarse fur,
Dark like smoke, or like shadow.
With her yearling next to her,
She ran out into the snow.

First the black wolf checked her pup,
Licked her nose and cuddled near.
Then she took a long jump up,
Trying hard the fence to clear.

Since she couldn't jump the wire,
She tried digging, tried to bite.
Pacing, she began to tire,
And by dawn, gave up the fight.

Just before the sun's first rays,
In the snow the black curled up.
Right beside her, in a daze,
Was her small, gray yearling pup.

Most wolves slept and hid all day.
But when purple shadows fell,
Black wolf would come out to play
With the pup she loved so well.

Then they tumbled, tossed and rolled,
Growled and barked and then touched noses.
You might think, if you weren't told,
Those were truly battle poses.

One day black wolf raised her head,
Turned her nose and sniffed the air,
Smelled an elk, just newly dead,
By the fencing, lying there.

Black wolf and the yearling ate,
Till they heard a sound begin.
Someone brought another crate,
With a large gray wolf within.

He just stood and looked at first;
Didn't growl or lift his fur.
Watchers might have feared the worst,
Thinking he might fight with her.

He was handsome, proud and strong.
His gray face was masked in black.
Rangers hoped, before too long,
With the black he'd start a pack.

Black wolf snarled at the male.
Bending low, he seemed to say,
As he stretched and wagged his tail,
"Okay, you can have your way."

Then the black wolf licked his face,
Sniffed his fur, and seemed to smile.
They began to run and chase,
Playing in the snow awhile.

Watchers hoped that in the spring,
When the wolves were freed again,
May would come and May would bring
Pups inside a safe, warm den.

21

And when several weeks had passed,
Rangers opened up the gate.
You would think, that free at last,
Those wolves wouldn't hesitate.

But the wolves showed no desire
To run out or to explore.
Rangers came to cut the wire,
Make the wolves another door.

Weren't they shocked to turn and find,
Who else, but the great big gray?
He was out and right behind,
Howling, in a warning way.

He'd been in and out before,
Though no one had seen him then.
So the rangers left once more,
Left those wolves alone again.

$\mathcal{I}$t was dark, and it was snowing
When the three wolves left the pen.
People kept an eye out, knowing,
They might not be seen again.

Snowy hillsides warmed and thawed.
Rivers melted, skies were blue.
Near a wolf-kill, ravens cawed.
(Ravens feed on wolf-kills too.)

People worried with each day.
But it wasn't long until
Someone saw the black and gray
Feeding on a new elk-kill.

And the younger wolf, alone,
Also seemed to be just fine.
She was roaming Yellowstone,
Independent, for a time.

Spring out west can come and go,
Icy winds can gust and sigh.
Sudden storms brought stinging snow.
Branches cracked and drifts blew high.

Early May brought awful news:
Gray wolf's collar had been found.
There was no one to accuse.
There was not a clue around.

Black wolf searched and found a space
Where spruce branches swept the snow.
There she made a hiding place,
In a shallow bowl below.

All alone, and with no help,
She gave birth to eight small pups,
No one near to see her whelp,
No one to help bring them up.

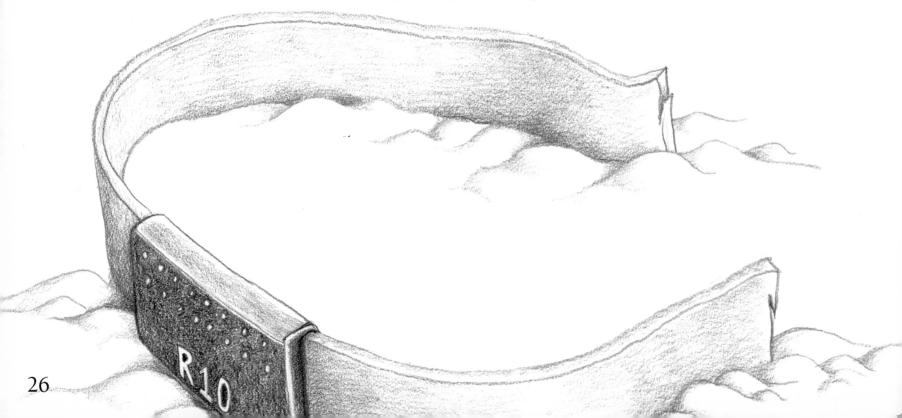

Mountain lions were a threat
With no pack to guard the pups.
Rangers didn't want to let
Any lion eat them up.

So the black was caught again.
(It was hard this time to hold her.)
With her pups in Rose Creek pen
She would stay till they were older.

When the wolves are freed once more,
When the pups hunt with the black,
Yearling pup, who left before,
May come back to join their pack.

Black wolf licks each tiny muzzle.
One small gray pup wags his tail.
Is the father any puzzle?
He's just like the proud gray male.

29

And in nineteen ninety-five
There were wolves in Yellowstone.
It is hoped that they will thrive,
Wolves in packs, and wolves alone.

There are wolves of silver gray:
There are wolves with masks of black.
They are shy, and run away,
But you just might see a track.

30

And beneath a lemon moon,
You might hear them in the park,
As they sing their longing tune,
When the night is velvet dark.

31

Glossary

Yellowstone	the first U.S. National Park, located in Wyoming
Pack	a wolf 'family', often with the mother and father and grown offspring working together to raise pups and hunt
Coyote	a shaggy, tan member of the dog family, smaller than a wolf
Bison, pronghorn	(also moose and deer) – all are wild animals, long legged, with hooves (called 'ungulates')
Haunting	something mysterious that stays in the mind
Predators	animals that kill and eat other animals
Stock	livestock: animals raised for meat and clothing (cattle, sheep)
Slain	killed
Endangered (Endangered List)	species in danger of extinction, with few remaining, are listed on 'The Endangered List'
Drone	a low, repetitive humming sound (like a motor)
Rangers	people who work for a National Park
Bolted	ran out fast
Yearling	a year old pup
Pacing	walking repeatedly back and forth
Poses	studied positions, not real but acting
Hesitate	wait a little bit
Whelp	give birth to pups

A Yellowstone wolf pup

Note: A few weeks after the gray male's collar was found, the hunter who shot and killed him was arrested. He faces up to a year in prison at the time of printing this book.

For those wishing to contact the Yellowstone Wolf Recovery Fund: P.O. Box 117, Yellowstone National Park, WY 82190. (307) 344-2293

The Humane Society of the U.S., a nonprofit organization founded in 1954, and with a constituency of over two million persons, is dedicated to speaking for animals, who cannot speak for themselves. The HSUS is devoted to making the world safe for animals through legal, educational, legislative and investigative means. The HSUS believes that humans have a moral obligation to protect other species with which we share the Earth. Co-sponsorship of this book by The Humane Society of the United States does not imply any partnership, joint venture, or other direct affiliation between The HSUS and Yellowstone National Park. For information on The HSUS, call: (202) 452-1100.

Text & Illustrations Copyright © 1995 by Randy Houk
Printed by Horowitz Rae
Designed by: Anita Soos Design, Inc.

ISBN 1-882728-25-4
Printed in the U.S.A.
Printed on recycled paper
10 9 8 7 6 5 4 3 2 1

Published by The Benefactory, Inc. One Post Road, Fairfield, CT 06430 The Benefactory produces books, tapes and toys that foster animal protection and environmental preservation. Call: (203) 255-7744

THE BENEFACTORY